Letts

KS2

Success

SATs

Maths

Jason White

Contents

Shape

Measures

Data

Notes

Answers

Place value and ordering

Place value

Digits can represent different numbers, depending on where you put them.

m	hth	tth	th	h	t	u
				4	3	2

This number is *four* hundred and *thirty-two*.

m	hth	tth	th	h	t	u
			8	0	1	7

This number is *eight* thousand and *seventeen*.

m	hth	tth	th	h	t	u
	4	9	1	2	0	7

This number is *four* hundred and *ninety-one* thousand, *two* hundred and *seven*.

key

u – units
t – tens
h – hundreds
th – thousands
tth – ten thousands
hth – hundred thousands
m – millions

SATs practice

 Write these numbers in order of size, starting with the smallest.

611   161   601   960   1016

smallest   largest

 Calculate...

1408 + 57 + 294

 What number is two hundred less than eleven thousand?

Ordering numbers

When ordering numbers, look carefully at the place value of each digit.

m	hth	tth	th	h	t	u	m	hth	tth	th	h	t	u
	6	4	2	3	0	0		6	4	1	8	9	4

There are;
6 hundred **th**ousands
4 ten **th**ousands
2 **th**ousands
3 **h**undreds
0 **t**ens and 0 **u**nits

There are;
6 hundred **th**ousands
4 ten **th**ousands
1 **th**ousands
8 **h**undreds
9 **t**ens and 4 **u**nits

The number *642,300* is greater than *641,894* because the first number has 2 thousands and the second number has only 1 thousand.

SATs practice

 What does the circled digit represent in this number?
Tick the correct answer.

7,4⑤8,634

5 hundreds ☐   5 millions ☐

5 thousands ☐   5 ten thousands ☐

 Put the following numbers in order, starting with the largest.
345,427   534,240   345,897   453,110

largest   smallest

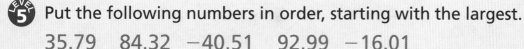 Put the following numbers in order, starting with the largest.
35.79   84.32   −40.51   92.99   −16.01

largest   smallest

Rounding and approximating

Rounding

We round numbers in order to make them easier to work with.

It is particularly useful for checking whether or not an answer is approximately correct.

Rounding to the nearest 10:

Number	Nearest 10
7	10
36	40
81	80
129	130
245	250
1,274	1,270
37,060	37,060

Remember:
Always round up if the number ends in 5, 6, 7, 8 or 9.

Always round down if the number ends in 1, 2, 3 or 4.

If the number ends in zero, it stays the same.

Rounding to the nearest 100:

Number	Nearest 100
64	100
329	300
452	500
2,874	2,900
7,059	7,100
17,218	17,200

Remember:
Always round up if the **tens** are 50, 60, 70, 80 or 90.

Always round down if the **tens** are 0, 10, 20, 30 or 40.

If the number ends in 00, it stays the same.

Rounding to the nearest 1000:

Number	Nearest 1000
581	1000
2,306	2,000
6,729	7,000
25,028	25,000
48,832	49,000
126,001	126,000
453,608	454,000

Remember:
Always round up if the **hundreds** are 500, 600, 700, 800 or 900.

Always round down if the **hundreds** are 0,100, 200, 300 or 400.

If the number ends in 000, it stays the same.

SATs practice

 Round the following numbers to the **nearest 10**.

37   73   95   128   202

 Round the following numbers to the **nearest 100**.

746   1,207   7,050   11,384   2,901

 Write the answer to the following calculations to the **nearest 10**.

(you may use a calculator)	To the **nearest 10**
74 × 13.4	
(13.6 − 9.25) × 128.6	
2,784 ÷ 83.72	

Rounding and approximating

Approximating

Approximating is another word for estimating.

Once you know how to round numbers, approximating is easy, as the numbers you are working with become more manageable.

Approximating is all about having a good guess. Look at the information you are given and try to work out what the answer will roughly be.

Example

Estimate the amount of water in the container.

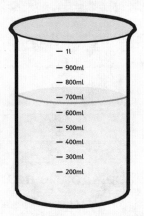

We need to look at the level of water against the scale and have a good guess at the amount in the jug.

Answer: A good guess would be 660ml or 670ml.

Now practise approximating.

SATs practice

 Estimate the amount of water in the jug.

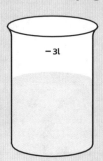

Jake can hop 37 metres in 1 minute. Estimate the distance Jake could hop in 50 minutes.

This is a working out box.

| | metres |

 A football club sold an average of 53,649 tickets per match during the season. The club played 22 games in the season. Estimate the total number of tickets sold during the season.

This is a working out box.

| | tickets |

Number patterns

Sequences

A number sequence is a list of numbers which follows a pattern.

Example

1, 5, 9, 13, 17, 21

This number sequence has a pattern of adding 4 more each time.

SATs practice

 Work out the next two numbers in this sequence.

9	16	23	30		

 Work out the next two numbers in this sequence.

7	14	28	56		

 Work out the two missing numbers in this sequence.

	7	15		63	127

More SATs practice

 Work out the next two numbers in this sequence.

43	35	27	19		

 Work out the next two numbers in this sequence.

96	48	24	12		

 Work out the next two numbers in this sequence.

408	200	96	44		

Negative numbers

Negative numbers are numbers which are below zero, as opposed to positive numbers which are above zero. You can see this easily on a thermometer, which is just like a number line.

The reading on this thermometer is 12°C. If the temperature drops by 20°C, the new temperature is −8°C. We have just counted back 20 places along the 'number line'.

SATs practice

 Work out the next number in this sequence.

16	11	6	1	−4	

 Work out the missing number in this sequence.

−23	−15		1	9	17

5 The temperature in Manchester on a day in July is 23°C. The temperature in the same place on a day in December is −9°C. What is the difference in the two temperatures?

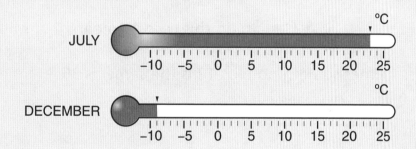

	°

Formulae and equations

Formulae and equations

A formula or an equation is a way of explaining a rule.

Sometimes you have to work out an equation to explain a rule.

Example

There are 120 seats at a music festival.

If *n seats* are sold, what equation shows how many seats are left?

Answer:

$$s = 120 - n \quad \text{where } \textbf{s} \text{ is the number of seats left}$$

Sometimes you have to look at an equation and work out what a symbol represents.

Example

$$4\textbf{n} + 12 = 36 \text{ (in this case } 4\textbf{n} \text{ means } 4 \times \textbf{n}\text{)}$$

In words: 4 times something plus 12 is the same as 36.

Answer:

$$\textbf{n} = 6 \qquad ((4 \times \textbf{6}) + 12 = 36)$$

More formulae and equations

Now practise using formulae and equations.

SATs practice

 Look at the following equation:

$163 - n = 147$

What is the value of n?

$n =$ ⬚

 Look at the following equation:

$s = 3n + 7$

If $n = 5$, what is the value of s?

$s =$ ⬚

 Look at the following equation:

$z + y = 46$

z is 10 more than y

Calculate the values of z and y.

$z =$ ⬚ $y =$ ⬚

Factors and multiples

Factors

A factor is any whole number which will divide exactly into another whole number.

Example

The factors of 20 are: 1, 20, 2, 10, 4, 5.

$$20 \div 1 = 20$$

$$20 \div 20 = 1$$

$$20 \div 2 = 10$$

$$20 \div 10 = 2$$

$$20 \div 4 = 5$$

$$20 \div 5 = 4$$

SATs practice

LEVEL 3 Work out the missing factors in these calculations.

$36 \div \boxed{} = 4$

$42 \div \boxed{} = 7$

$64 \div \boxed{} = 32$

LEVEL 4 Write down all the factors of 32.

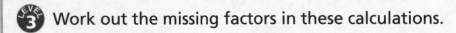

LEVEL 5 Circle all the numbers which have a factor of 7.

49   72   117   147   28   84

Multiples

A multiple is any number made by multiplying two numbers together.

20 is a multiple of 5 because 4 × 5 = 20.

69 is a multiple of 3 because 23 × 3 = 69.

SATs practice

LEVEL 3 Write down 3 multiples of 6.

☐ ☐ ☐

LEVEL 4 Circle the multiples of 9.

81   99   69   45   27   199

LEVEL 5 Write down 3 multiples of both 4 and 5.

☐ ☐ ☐

More SATs practice

LEVEL 3 Write down 3 multiples of 7.

☐ ☐ ☐

LEVEL 4 Circle the multiples of 8.

16   68   88   40   18   184

LEVEL 5 Write down 3 multiples of both 6 and 5.

☐ ☐ ☐

Fractions

Types of fractions

A fraction is made up of two numbers.

The numerator is the top number in the fraction.
The denominator is the bottom number in the fraction.

Example

$$\frac{2}{3} \begin{array}{l} - \text{ numerator} \\ - \text{ denominator} \end{array}$$

There are three types of fractions.

A **proper fraction**, where the numerator is smaller than the denominator.

e.g. $\frac{2}{3}$

An **improper fraction**, where the numerator is larger than the denominator.

e.g. $\frac{7}{3}$

A **mixed number fraction**, which consists of whole numbers and a proper fraction.

e.g. $8\frac{2}{3}$

SATs practice

 Circle the improper fraction below.

$\frac{7}{10}$ $\frac{3}{4}$ $\frac{4}{2}$ $\frac{9}{15}$ $\frac{1}{7}$

 Write down a mixed number fraction between 1 and 10.

Equivalent fractions

Equivalent fractions are fractions that have the same value – that are **equal**.

Example

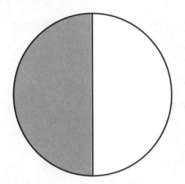

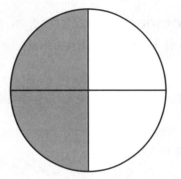

This circle has $\frac{1}{2}$ shaded in green.

This circle has $\frac{2}{4}$ shaded in green which is equivalent to $\frac{1}{2}$.

So $\frac{1}{2}$ and $\frac{2}{4}$ are equivalent fractions.

SATs practice

 Here is a rectangle.

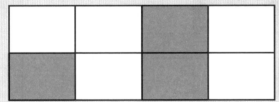

What fraction of the rectangle is shaded?

 Write a fraction that is equivalent to each of the following decimals.

0.25 _____

0.5 _____

0.125 _____

0.875 _____

 Write an improper fraction that is equivalent to each of the following decimals.

1.4 _____

3.125 _____

10.8 _____

5.02 _____

Fractions

Comparing fractions

When comparing fractions, all you need to think about is whether one fraction is bigger than another fraction.

It is quite clear in the diagram below that $\frac{1}{2}$ is greater than $\frac{1}{4}$.

Also $\frac{2}{3}$ is less than $\frac{6}{8}$.

1 whole

$\frac{1}{2}$	$\frac{2}{2}$

$\frac{1}{4}$	$\frac{2}{4}$	$\frac{3}{4}$	$\frac{4}{4}$

$\frac{1}{3}$	$\frac{2}{3}$	$\frac{3}{3}$

$\frac{1}{6}$	$\frac{2}{6}$	$\frac{3}{6}$	$\frac{4}{6}$	$\frac{5}{6}$	$\frac{6}{6}$

$\frac{1}{8}$	$\frac{2}{8}$	$\frac{3}{8}$	$\frac{4}{8}$	$\frac{5}{8}$	$\frac{6}{8}$	$\frac{7}{8}$	$\frac{8}{8}$

$\frac{1}{2}$　　　　$\frac{1}{4}$　　　　　　$\frac{2}{3}$　　　　$\frac{6}{8}$

SATs practice

Now practise what you have learnt.

 Put a circle around the largest fraction of the following pairs.

$\frac{1}{3}$ $\frac{2}{8}$

$\frac{1}{5}$ $\frac{1}{3}$

$\frac{2}{7}$ $\frac{1}{9}$

$\frac{5}{8}$ $\frac{3}{6}$

$\frac{2}{3}$ $\frac{1}{10}$

$\frac{1}{9}$ $\frac{3}{8}$

 Put these fractions in order, starting with the largest.

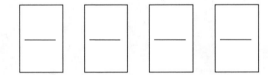

$\frac{4}{5}$ $\frac{1}{3}$ $\frac{3}{4}$ $\frac{1}{2}$

—	—	—	—

largest   smallest

 Put these fractions in order, starting with the largest.

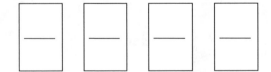

$\frac{9}{10}$ $\frac{1}{4}$ $\frac{4}{7}$ $\frac{13}{18}$

—	—	—	—

largest   smallest

Decimals

Decimals

A decimal is a number that lies between two whole numbers, like a fraction.

All decimals are equal to one or more fractions.

$\frac{1}{2} = 0.5$ $2\frac{1}{2} = 2.5$ $3\frac{1}{2} = 3.5$

$\frac{1}{4} = 0.25$ $2\frac{1}{4} = 2.25$ $3\frac{3}{4} = 3.75$

Some fractions have recurring decimals.

$\frac{1}{3} = 0.3333....$ $\frac{2}{3} = 0.6666....$

$2\frac{1}{3} = 2.3333....$ $4\frac{2}{3} = 4.6666....$

SATs practice

 What fraction is equivalent to 0.8? _____

 What is double 3.7? _____

 Work out 2.3 multiplied by 4. Write your answer as a fraction.

Comparing decimals

In order to compare decimals, we need to understand what each digit represents.

43.67	43.7
4 represents 4 tens	4 represents 4 tens
3 represents 3 units	3 represents 3 units
6 represents 6 tenths	7 represents 7 tenths
7 represents 7 hundredths	

The decimal 43.7 is greater than 43.67, because it has more tenths. We can think of this as 43.70 because there are zero hundredths!

Always compare numbers from the left-hand side to the right-hand side. In our example, the tens are the same, the units are the same, but the tenths are different, so whichever has the greater number of tenths must be the largest number.

SATs practice

 Circle the decimals that are greater than $\frac{1}{2}$.

0.2   0.53   0.75   0.45   0.12

 Put the correct sign (< or >) between the following numbers.

4.5	☐	4.56
9.42	☐	9.09
26.89	☐	26.9

 Write these decimals in order. The first one has been done for you.

6.04   6.4   6.24   6.42   6.02   6.2   6

6						

smallest   largest

21

Percentages

Percentages

A percentage is just a different way of writing a fraction.

10%	25%	50%
is just the same as	is just the same as	is just the same as
$\frac{10}{100}$ or even $\frac{1}{10}$	$\frac{25}{100}$ or even $\frac{1}{4}$	$\frac{50}{100}$ or $\frac{5}{10}$ or $\frac{1}{2}$

Example

50% of £10 = £5

$\frac{1}{2}$ of £10 = £5

SATs practice

 Write $\frac{6}{10}$ as a percentage. _____

 What **percentage** of the grid below is shaded? _____

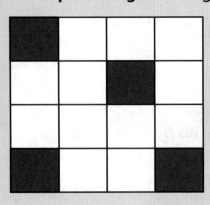

Decimals and percentages

Decimals and percentages are really the same thing; they are just written in different ways.

10%	25%	50%
is just the same as	is just the same as	is just the same as
0.1	0.25	0.5

Divide by 100 to get the equivalent decimal.

Similarly

0.23	0.78	0.9
is just the same as	is just the same as	is just the same as
23%	78%	90%

We just multiply by 100 to get the equivalent percentage.

SATs practice

 What is 0.4 written as a percentage? _____

 Write 84% as a decimal. _____

 Calculate 13% of 364.
You may use a calculator. _____

More SATs practice

 What is 0.75 written as a percentage? _____

 Write 9% as a decimal. _____

 Calculate 32% of £90.
You may use a calculator. _____

Ratio and proportion

Proportion

Proportion is comparing part of something to the whole of something. Finding a proportion of an amount is just like finding a fraction of an amount.

For instance, to ask "What proportion of the class has blue eyes?" is the same as to ask "What fraction of the class has blue eyes?"

Two fractions can also be said to be in proportion to each other.

Example

A score of 4 out of 5 would be in proportion to a score of 8 out of 10.

$$4:5 = 8:10 \quad \text{or } \frac{4}{5} = \frac{8}{10}$$

The answer would be the same in both cases.

SATs practice

 What proportion of this square is shaded? Write your answer as a fraction.

_____

 There are 32 children in Class 7. In the class there are 20 girls. What proportion of the class are boys?

Ratio

A ratio compares the value of one or more amounts with another. A score of 4 out of 5 may be written as 4:5 or as a fraction $\frac{4}{5}$.

Example

If it takes 8 oranges to make 1 litre of orange juice, then it would take 16 oranges to make 2 litres of juice, and 24 oranges to make 3 litres … and so on.

This is a ratio of 8:1 (8 oranges per 1 litre).

SATs practice

 In a box of six eggs, there are 2 brown eggs and 4 white eggs. What is the ratio of brown eggs to white eggs?

_____

 It takes 8 apples and 24 blackberries to make two apple and blackberry pies. What is the ratio of apples to blackberries in one pie?

Mental maths

Number bonds to 20

Number bonds are common pairs of numbers that equal another number, in this case 20.

Knowing your number bonds to 20 will help you with mental maths – doing calculations in your head.

Example

$4 + 8 = 12$

and the reverse of this is

$12 - 8 = 4$ or $12 - 4 = 8$

$6 + 7 = 13$

$13 - 6 = 7$

+	0	1	2	3	4	5	6	7	8	9	10
0	0	1	2	3	4	5	6	7	8	9	10
1	1	2	3	4	5	6	7	8	9	10	11
2	2	3	4	5	6	7	8	9	10	11	12
3	3	4	5	6	7	8	9	10	11	12	13
4	4	5	6	7	8	9	10	11	12	13	14
5	5	6	7	8	9	10	11	12	13	14	15
6	6	7	8	9	10	11	12	13	14	15	16
7	7	8	9	10	11	12	13	14	15	16	17
8	8	9	10	11	(12)	13	14	15	16	17	18
9	9	10	11	12	13	14	15	16	17	18	19
10	10	11	12	13	14	15	16	17	18	19	20

Ideally, you should know all the number bonds to 20 off by heart.

Now practise what you have learnt.

SATs practice

(3) Add together six, eight and five.

_____

(4) Add together nought point five, nought point seven and nought point three.

_____

(5) Write down two factors of thirty-two which add together to make twenty.

_____ + _____ = 20

More SATs practice

(3) Add together four, nine and three.

_____

(4) Add together nought point eight, nought point five and nought point two.

_____

(5) Write down two factors of eighteen which multiply together to make twelve.

_____ × _____ = 12

Mental maths

Adding 2-digit numbers

When doing mental addition with larger numbers, always hold the bigger of the two numbers in your head. Then add first the tens, then the units of the smaller number to it.

Example

$$46 + 28 = ?$$
$$46 + 20 = 66$$
and $66 + 8 = 74$
so $46 + 28 = 74$

SATs practice

3 Add together fifty-three and forty. ☐

4 Add together sixty-eight and twenty-seven. ☐

5 Add together twenty-two point four, and thirty-nine point seven.
☐

More SATs practice

3 Add together fifty and thirty-six. ☐

4 Add together eighty-four and seventy-nine. ☐

5 Add together fifty-six point eight, and twenty-seven point seven.
☐

Subtracting 2-digit numbers

An easy way to do mental subtraction is to find the difference. Simply count on from the smaller number to the bigger one.

Example

$84 - 38 = ?$

$38 + 2 = 40$	added 2
$40 + 40 = 80$	added 40
$80 + 4 = 84$	added 4

Then total up all the numbers you added.

$2 + 40 + 4 = 46$

so

$84 - 38 = 46$

SATs practice

 Subtract twenty from forty-three. ☐

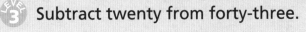 Subtract thirty-seven from ninety-two. ☐

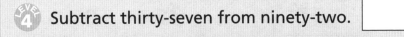 Calculate the difference between four hundred and seventy-nine and five hundred and forty-three.

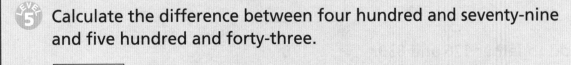

☐

Addition and subtraction

Addition

The most common way of doing written addition is the column method.

Example

238 + 147 = ?

First, make sure that the units, tens and
hundreds are in columns underneath each other.

```
  238
 +147
```

Then add the units.	Then add the tens.	Lastly, add the hundreds.
238	238	238
+147	+147	+147
5	85	385
1	1	1

This works exactly the same with bigger numbers and with decimals. Just remember, **always** keep the digits in the correct columns and **always** add from the right and work your way left until all the digits have been added.

SATs practice

3 Add together 37 and 94.

```
  37
 +94
```

[ ]

4 Add together 176 and 839.

```
  176
 +839
```

[ ]

5 Add together 371.84 and 4,643.09.

[ ]

Subtraction

The column method is also the most common way of doing written subtraction.

Example

746 − 452 = ?

Again, make sure that the units, tens and hundreds are in columns underneath each other.

```
  746
 −452
```

Then subtract the units.

Then subtract the tens, remembering to exchange 1 hundred for 10 tens.

Lastly, subtract the hundreds.

```
  7 4 6
 −4 5 2
      4
```

```
  7 4 6
 −4 5 2
    9 4
```

```
  ⁶7 ¹⁴4 6
 −4  5 2
   2 9 4
```

SATs practice

 Subtract 34 from 78.

```
   78
  −34
```

 Subtract 187 from 562.

```
  562
 −187
```

Calculate the difference between 387 and 5,234.

Multiplication

Grid method

There are two main methods you can use to do a multiplication sum. The first of these is the grid method.

As the name implies, this involves using a grid.

Example

$37 \times 64 = ?$

First, partition, or split up, both numbers into tens and units and put them on the outside of the grid, 37 (30 + 7) on the left and 64 (60 + 4) on the top.

$\times$	60	4	Total
30			
7			

Then fill in the boxes by doing the simple multiplication sums, 30×60, 30×4, 7×60 and 7×4.

Then put the answers into the correct boxes.

$\times$	60	4	Total
30	1800	120	1920
7	420	28	+ 448
			2368

Add up the totals from the two rows and get the answer 2368.

Now practise using the grid method.

3 A box holds 24 cans. If there are 7 boxes of cans, how many cans are there altogether?

24 CANS

	cans

4 In a multi-pack there are 24 bags of crisps. Jayne buys 16 multi-packs for the party. How many bags of crisps has she bought altogether?

	bags

5 Calculate 374 × 68.

Multiplication

Column method

The other method of doing multiplication sums is called the column method. It uses partitioning in much the same way as the grid method, but sets it out differently.

Example

$37 \times 64 = ?$

Write it out
like this

$$
\begin{array}{r}
37 \\
\times\ 64 \\
\hline
\end{array}
$$

Multiply the units first.

$$
\begin{array}{r}
37 \\
\times\ 4 \\
\end{array}
\qquad\text{or}\qquad
\begin{array}{r}
37 \\
\times\ 4 \\
\end{array}
$$

$(4 \times 7) \longrightarrow 28 \qquad\qquad 148$

$(4 \times 30) \longrightarrow \underline{120} \qquad\qquad {}_2$

$\qquad\qquad\qquad 148$

Now multiply the tens.

$$
\begin{array}{r}
37 \\
\times\ 60 \\
\end{array}
$$

$(60 \times 7) \longrightarrow 420$

$(60 \times 30) \longrightarrow \underline{1800}$

$\qquad\qquad\qquad 2220$

Now add the two answers together.

$$
\begin{array}{r}
148 \\
+2220 \\
\hline
2368
\end{array}
\qquad\text{or}\qquad
\begin{array}{r}
37 \\
\times\ 64 \\
\hline
148 \\
2220 \\
\hline
2368
\end{array}
$$

Now practise using the column method.

SATs practice

3 There are 6 eggs in a box. How many eggs are there in 38 boxes?

eggs

4 At a secondary school there are 28 children in each class. There are 39 classes in the school. How many children are there altogether?

children

5 Calculate 83 × 467.

Division

Long division

Division is just the opposite of multiplication.

$7 \times 8 = 56$ so $56 \div 8 = 7$ and $56 \div 7 = 8$

You can write division out like this too.

$$7 \overline{)56}^{8}$$

When dividing a large number, you can use long division.

Example

$376 \div 8 = ?$ All we do is count back in 8s until we get to zero.

```
          47
    8 |  376
       -  80  ← (10 x 8)
          296
       -  80  ← (10 x 8)
          216
       -  80  ← (10 x 8)
          136
       -  80  ← (10 x 8)
          56
       -  56  ← (7 x 8)
          00
```

Once we have counted all the way back to zero, we need to add up the total lots of 8, i.e. $10 + 10 + 10 + 10 + 7 = 47$, so, $376 \div 8 = \mathbf{47}$

This is rather a long-winded way of doing it and it can be reduced by putting all the jumps of 10×8 together.

```
          47
    8 |  376
       - 320  ← (40 x 8)
          56
       -  56  ← (7 x 8)
          00
```

Or even shorter like this:

```
          47
    8 | 376
          5
```

$40 + 7 = \mathbf{47}$

SATs practice

There are 102 seats in the cinema and 6 rows. How many seats are there in a row?

seats

Mr Green has £441. He would like to give each of his 7 grandchildren an equal share of the money. How much money will each child get?

£

Calculate £2560 ÷ 8.

£

Division

Remainders

Sometimes one number will not divide exactly into another number. When this happens, we have some left over. This leftover amount is called the 'remainder'.

Example

If I shared 13 sweets between 4 people, they would get 3 each and there would be 1 left. This 1 is the remainder.

Example

$379 \div 8 = ?$

```
      47 r3
  8 │ 379
    – 320 ←(40 x 8)
      59
    –  56 ← (7 x 8)
      03
```

Now, 40 + 7 = 47 remainder 3

SAT's practice

 Calculate and find the remainder. $93 \div 5 = ?$

6 friends shared 212 sweets equally. How many sweets did they get each and how many were left over?

sweets each	sweets left

Some people go on a cruise from the first of September until the end of July the following year. How many days do they cruise for, providing it is not a leap year? How many whole weeks do they cruise for?

days cruising	weeks cruising

Problems with fractions

About fractions

There are lots of problems that involve the use of fractions, so you need to make sure that you really understand the basics.

$\dfrac{2}{3}$ – numerator
– denominator

Example 1

Find $\frac{2}{3}$ of 24.

First, find $\frac{1}{3}$ of 24, which is the same as $24 \div 3$.

So $\frac{1}{3}$ of 24 = 8

$\frac{2}{3}$ is just $\frac{1}{3} + \frac{1}{3}$

So $\frac{2}{3}$ of 24 = 8 + 8 = 16.

Example 2

Find $\frac{3}{4}$ of 48.

First, find $\frac{1}{4}$ of 48, which is the same as $48 \div 4$.

So $\frac{1}{4}$ of 48 = 12 $\frac{3}{4}$ is just $\frac{1}{4} + \frac{1}{4} + \frac{1}{4}$

Answer: $\frac{3}{4}$ of 48 = 12 + 12 + 12 = 36.

Now practise what you have learnt.

3 Find $\frac{1}{4}$ of 32.

4 Calculate $\frac{4}{5}$ of £30.

£

5 What is $\frac{3}{4}$ of £88?

£

Problems with fractions

More problems with fractions

Word problems sometimes cause confusion, especially when fractions are involved. You need to read the question really carefully and try to work out what calculation it is that you need to do.

Example

John had a box with 24 chocolates in it. Two thirds of the chocolates had soft centres. Write down the number of chocolates with soft centres in the box.

Although this seems complicated, the sum you need to do is...

$\frac{2}{3}$ of 24 = ?

which we did earlier in this section. The answer is 16.

Now practise doing some word problems.

SATs practice

3 Sarah has £10. She spends $\frac{1}{4}$ of her money. How much has she spent?

£

4 Holly goes to the cinema and spends $\frac{2}{3}$ of her money. She took £15 with her. How much money does she have left?

£

5 Five sixths of a number is 120. What is the number?

Problems with percentages

Percentages of an amount

Finding the percentage of an amount is a common step in many maths problems.

Remember that percentages are just another way of writing fractions. If you can work out a fraction of an amount, you can work out a percentage of an amount.

Example

20% of £30 is the same as $\frac{20}{100}$ of £30

or $\frac{2}{10}$ of £30, or even $\frac{1}{5}$ of £30.

SATs practice

 Calculate 30% of 15kg.

kg

 What is 45% of £95?

£

Percentage change

A percentage change is when a quantity increases or decreases by a certain amount.

Example

A dress costs £12. It is reduced by 10% in the sale. What is the cost of the dress in the sale?

First, you need to find out the amount the dress has been reduced by.	Then you need to **subtract** this amount from the original price to find your answer.	If the dress was increasing in price, we would **add** the 10% to the original price.
10% of £12 = £1.20	£12 − £1.20 = £10.80	£12 + £1.20 = £13.20

SATs practice

 A shop sells computer games for £20. There is a sale on and games are reduced by 10%. How much does a game cost in the sale?

£

 At the garden centre 1000kg of sand costs £85. If you buy 4000kg of sand, you get a 10% discount in the price. How much does 4000kg of sand cost?

£

2D shapes

2D shapes

A 2D or two-dimensional shape is a flat shape having only two dimensions, which are length and breadth.

There are many different types of 2D shapes, all with different names and properties. Here are just some of them.

Polygons

Polygons are any 2D shapes with all straight sides. In a **regular polygon**, the sides and the angles are all the same size. An **irregular polygon** has one or more sides or angles that are different to the others.

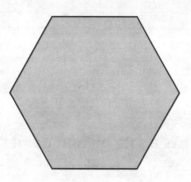
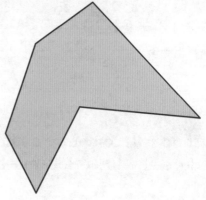

Regular Polygon   Irregular Polygon

Triangles

A triangle is a 3-sided 2D polygon.

An **equilateral triangle** has 3 equal length sides and equal angles.

An **isosceles triangle** has 2 equal length sides and 2 equal angles.

A **scalene triangle** has 0 equal length sides and 0 equal angles.

A **right-angled triangle** has one 90° angle (L-shaped).

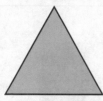

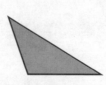

Equilateral   Isosceles   Scalene   Right-angled
Triangle   Triangle   Triangle   Triangle

Now practise what you have learnt about 2D shapes.

SATs practice

 An isosceles triangle has _____ sides the same length.

A regular octagon has _____ sides.

An irregular hexagon has _____ sides.

An equilateral triangle has _____ equal length sides.

A rectangle has _____ right angles.

An irregular polygon has _____ curved sides.

 An equilateral triangle has a perimeter measuring 90cm. How long is each side?

_____ cm

Here are four statements. Put a (✓) if the statement is correct, or a (✗) if the statement is incorrect.

An irregular polygon does not have straight sides. ☐

An isosceles triangle has 2 equal angles. ☐

A right-angled triangle can sometimes be an equilateral triangle. ☐

An equilateral triangle has 3 acute angles. ☐

2D shapes

2D shape problems

Quadrilaterals are four-sided polygons. There are many different types of quadrilaterals, all of which have special properties.

Example

A **square** has 4 equal length sides and 4 right angles. A square also has 2 pairs of parallel sides.

A **rectangle** has 2 pairs of equal length sides and 4 right angles. A rectangle also has 2 pairs of parallel sides.

A **parallelogram** has opposite sides of equal length and parallel.

Examples of other quadrilaterals are a kite, a rhombus and a trapezium.

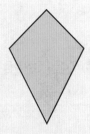 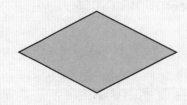 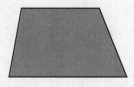

Note – *Parallel sides*

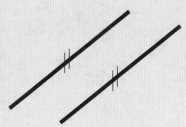  

All these are pairs of parallel sides. Just think of railway tracks!

Maths answer booklet

NUMBERS

PLACE VALUE AND ORDERING

PAGE 4 Place value
SATs practice
❸ 161 601 611 960 1016
❹ 1,759
❺ 10,800

PAGE 5 Ordering numbers
SATs Practice
❸ 5 ten thousands
❹ 534,240 453,110 345,897 345,427
❺ 92.99 84.32 35.79 -16.01 -40.51

ROUNDING AND APPROXIMATING

PAGE 7 Rounding
SATs Practice
❸ 40 70 100 130 200
❹ 700 1,200 7,100 11,400 2,900
❺ (you may use a calculator)

	To the nearest 10
74 x 13.4	990
(13.6 – 9.25) x 128.6	560
2,784 ÷ 83.72	30

PAGE 8 Approximating
SATs Practice
❸ Answers in the range 2.2l – 2.3l, or 2200ml – 2300ml.
❹ Answers in the range 1700m – 2000m.
❺ Answers in the range 1,100,000 – 1,210,000 tickets.

NUMBER PATTERNS

PAGE 10 Sequences
SATs Practice
❸ 9 16 23 30 **37** **44**
❹ 7 14 28 56 **112** **224**
❺ 3 7 15 **31** 63 127

More SATs Practice
❸ 43 35 27 19 **11** 3
❹ 96 48 24 12 **6** 3
❺ 408 200 96 44 **18** 5

PAGE 11 Negative numbers
SATs Practice
❸ 16 11 6 1 -4 **-9**
❹ -23 -15 **-7** 1 9 17
❺ 32°C

FORMULAE AND EQUATIONS

PAGE 13 Formulae and equations
SATs Practice
❸ n = 16
❹ s = 22
❺ z = 28 and y = 18

FACTORS AND MULTIPLES

PAGE 14 Factors
SATs Practice
❸ 9, 6, 2
❹ 1, 2, 4, 8, 16, 32
❺ (49) 72 117 (147) (28) (84)

PAGE 15 Multiples
SATs Practice
❸ Any 3 numbers which divide by 6 exactly.
❹ (81) (99) 69 (45) (27) 199
❺ Any three numbers in the sequence 20, 40, 60, 80 etc.

More SATs Practice
❸ Any 3 numbers which divide by 7 exactly.
❹ (16) 68 (88) (40) 18 (184)
❺ Any three numbers in the sequence 30, 60, 90, 120 etc.

FRACTIONS

PAGE 16 Types of fractions
SATs Practice
❸ $\frac{7}{10}$ $\frac{3}{4}$ $(\frac{4}{2})$ $\frac{9}{15}$ $\frac{1}{7}$
❹ Any mixed number fraction from 1 – 10, eg. $4\frac{1}{2}$, $3\frac{1}{2}$, $9\frac{1}{10}$ etc.

PAGE 17 Equivalent fractions
SATs Practice
❸ $\frac{3}{8}$
❹ $\frac{1}{4}$ or $\frac{25}{100}$ $\frac{1}{2}$ or $\frac{5}{10}$ or $\frac{50}{100}$ etc., $\frac{1}{8}$ or $\frac{125}{1000}$ etc., $\frac{7}{8}$ or $\frac{875}{1000}$ etc.
❺ $\frac{14}{10}$ or $\frac{140}{100}$, $\frac{25}{8}$, $\frac{108}{10}$, $\frac{502}{100}$

PAGE 19 Comparing fractions
SATs Practice
❸ $(\frac{1}{3})$ $\frac{2}{8}$ $(\frac{5}{8})$ $\frac{3}{6}$
  $\frac{1}{5}$ $(\frac{1}{3})$ $(\frac{2}{3})$ $\frac{1}{10}$
  $(\frac{2}{7})$ $\frac{1}{9}$ $\frac{1}{9}$ $(\frac{3}{8})$
❹ largest $\frac{4}{5}$ $\frac{3}{4}$ $\frac{1}{2}$ $\frac{1}{3}$ smallest
❺ largest $\frac{9}{10}$ $\frac{13}{18}$ $\frac{4}{7}$ $\frac{1}{4}$ smallest

DECIMALS

PAGE 20 Decimals
SATs Practice
❸ $\frac{8}{10}$ or $\frac{4}{5}$
❹ 7.4
❺ $9\frac{2}{10}$ or $9\frac{1}{5}$

PAGE 21 Comparing decimals
SATs Practice
❸ 0.2 (0.53) (0.75) 0.45 0.12
❹ 4.5 < 4.56
  9.42 > 9.09
  26.89 < 26.9
❺ 6 6.02 6.04 6.2 6.24 6.4 6.42

PERCENTAGES

PAGE 22 Percentages
SATs Practice
❹ 60%
❺ 25%

PAGE 23 Decimals and percentages
SATs Practice
③ 40%
④ 0.84
⑤ 47.32
More SATs Practice
③ 75%
④ 0.09
⑤ £28.80

RATIO AND PROPORTION
PAGE 24 Proportion
SATs Practice
④ $\frac{3}{8}$ or $\frac{6}{16}$ or 3:8 or 6:16
⑤ $\frac{3}{8}$ or $\frac{6}{16}$ or $\frac{12}{32}$ or 3:8 or 6:16 or 12:32

PAGE 25 Ratio
SATs Practice
④ 1:2 or 2:4
⑤ 1:3 or 2:6   3:9 or 4:12

CALCULATIONS
MENTAL MATHS
PAGE 27 Number bonds to 20
SATs Practice
③ 19
④ 1.5
⑤ 16 and 4
More SATs Practice
③ 16
④ 1.5
⑤ 2 and 6

PAGE 28 Adding 2-digit numbers
SATs Practice
③ 93
④ 95
⑤ 62.1
More SATs Practice
③ 86
④ 163
⑤ 84.5

PAGE 29 Subtracting 2-digit numbers
SATs Practice
③ 23
④ 55
⑤ 64

ADDITION AND SUBTRACTION
PAGE 30 Addition
SATs Practice
③ 131
④ 1,015
⑤ 5,014.93

PAGE 31 Subtraction
SATs Practice
③ 44
④ 375
⑤ 4,847

MULTIPLICATION
PAGE 33 Grid method
SATs Practice
③ 168 cans (need to show workings)
④ 384 bags (need to show workings)
⑤ 25,432

PAGE 35 Column method
SATs Practice
③ 228
④ 1,092
⑤ 38,761

DIVISION
PAGE 37 Long division
SATs Practice
③ 17 seats
④ £63
⑤ £320

PAGE 38 Remainders
SATs Practice
③ 18 remainder 3
④ 35 sweets each, 2 sweets left
⑤ 334 days cruising, 47 weeks cruising

FRACTIONS
PAGE 41 About fractions
SATs Practice
③ 8
④ £24
⑤ £66

PAGE 43 More problems with fractions
SATs Practice
③ £2.50
④ £5
⑤ 144

PERCENTAGES
PAGE 44 Percentages of an amount
SATs Practice
④ 4.5kg
⑤ £42.75

PAGE 45 Percentage change
SATs Practice
④ £18
⑤ £306

SHAPE
PAGE 47 2D shapes
SATs Practice
③ 2, 8, 6, 3, 4, 0
④ 30cm
⑤ An irregular polygon does not have straight sides. ✗
An isosceles triangle has 2 equal angles. ✓
A right-angle triangle can sometimes be an equilateral triangle. ✗
An equilateral triangle has 3 acute angles. ✓

PAGE 49 2D shape problems
SATs Practice

③
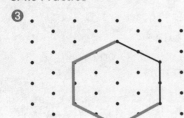

④
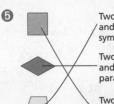
etc.

⑤

Two acute angles and no lines of symmetry.

Two acute angles and 2 pairs of parallel sides.

Two pairs of parallel sides and four lines of symmetry.

An area of less than six squares and no parallel sides.

3D SHAPES (SOLIDS)

PAGE 52 3D shapes (Solids)
SATs Practice

③ Number of faces
Cone 2
cube 6
sphere 1
cylinder 3

④
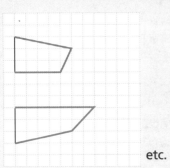

⑤ Any one of these three:
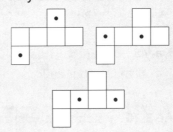

PAGE 53 3D shape problems
SATs Practice

③

	Number of faces	Number of edges
cone	2	1
cube	6	12
sphere	1	0
cylinder	3	2

④ 8

⑤

	Number of edges	Number of vertices
cuboid	12	8
square-based pyramid	8	5
triangular prism	9	6
tetrahedron	6	4

GEOMETRY

PAGE 54 Symmetry and reflection
SATs Practice

③
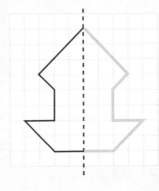

④
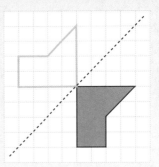

⑤ C (11 , 16)   D (17 , 8)

PAGE 56 Rotation and translation
SATs Practice

③
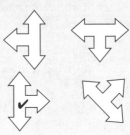

④

⑤
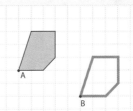

COORDINATES

PAGE 59 Basic coordinates
SATs Practice

③ A = (3 , 6)   B = (1 , 3)
C = (5 , 1)

④ (7 , 4)

⑤ C = (16 , 10)

PAGE 60 Advanced coordinates
SATs Practice

⑤ (1 , -4)

ANGLES

PAGE 62 Types of angles

SATs Practice

③ Any shape similar to these, with 2 right angles.

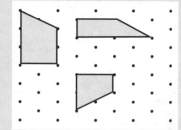

④ 55° (accept answers ranging from 50° to 60°)

⑤ 26°

PAGE 63 Measuring angles

SATs Practice

④ 115° (accept answers in the range 112° to 118°)

⑤ Check that the two angles are within 3° + or − of 40°

MEASURES

UNITS OF MEASURE

PAGE 65 Units of measure and converting

SATs Practice

③ 200cm

④ 750ml

⑤ 13 loaves

More SATs Practice

③ 4000kg

④ 370cl

⑤ 10 litres

READING SCALES

PAGE 67 Reading scales

SATs Practice

③ 1400ml

④ 260ml

⑤ a 175g

　 b 175g

TIME

PAGE 69 Time and the calendar

SATs Practice

③ a 48 hours,　b 61 days

④ a 17th October 2008

　 b Wednesday

PAGE 70 Analogue and digital time

SATs Practice

③

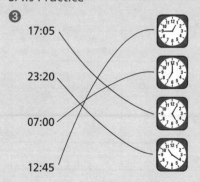

④ a 1 hour 35 minutes

　 b 4 hours 53 minutes

⑤ 8.05pm or 20.05 or five past eight at night

PERIMETER AND AREA

PAGE 73 Perimeter

SATs Practice

③ 187m

④ 7cm

⑤ 13.8cm

PAGE 75 Area

SATs Practice

③ 1 = 16 squares; 2 = 17 $\frac{1}{2}$ squares

④ Any rectangle with an area of 24 squares.

⑤ 208cm^2

DATA

PROBABILITY

PAGE 77 Chance and outcome

SATs Practice

③ white

④ 2 and 3

⑤ $\frac{2}{5}$ or $\frac{20}{50}$

TABLES, CHARTS AND GRAPHS

PAGE 78 Bar charts

SATs Practice

③ £7, £4

④ Approx 44 points, 2007, 30 points

⑤ a 150 secs

　 b 107 (accept 100-120)

PAGE 80 Picture graphs

SATs Practice

③ a 5 hours

　 b 11 hours

④ a 3400 (accept 3350-3450)

　 b 2100 (accept 2050-2150)

⑤ 1000 (accept 950-1050)

PAGE 83 Pie charts

SATs Practice

③ a $\frac{1}{6}$

　 b 15

PAGE 85 Line graphs

SATs Practice

④ 750m, 450m

⑤ 18.5°C (accept 18.3-18.7), 2:45pm

AVERAGES

PAGE 87 Mode

SATs Practice

④ Mode = 126cm

⑤ Mode = 1.25m

PAGE 88 Mean

SATs Practice

④ Mean = 6

⑤ Mean = 3

PAGE 89 Median

SATs Practice

④ Median = 108

⑤ Median = 14

SATs practice

 On the grid below, draw the other lines **4** lines which complete a **regular hexagon**.

Don't forget, you'll find it easier if you use a ruler!

 Look at the grid below.
Draw a quadrilateral with no parallel sides.

2D shapes

2D shape problems (continued)

 Match each of the shapes to the correct description.

One has been done for you

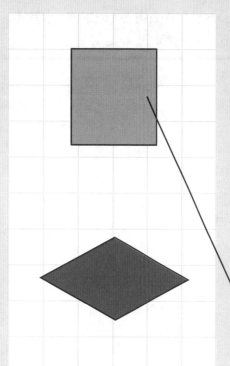

Two acute angles and no lines of symmetry.

Two acute angles and 2 pairs of parallel sides.

Two pairs of parallel sides and four lines of symmetry.

An area of less than 6 squares and no parallel sides.

3D shapes (solids)

3D shapes (solids)

A 3D or three-dimensional shape is a solid shape having three dimensions, which are length, breadth and height.

Another name for 3D shapes is solid shapes. There are lots of different sorts of 3D shapes.

Here are some of them.

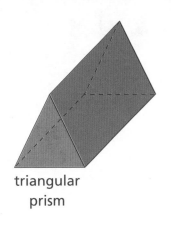

triangular
prism

cone

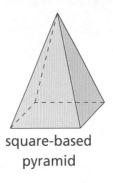

square-based
pyramid

tetrahedron

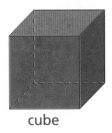

cube

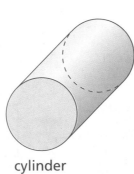

cylinder

sphere

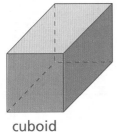

cuboid

You will need to know the names and properties of all these shapes.

3D shapes (solids)

3D shapes (solids) (continued)

A net is what a 3D shape looks like when it is opened up flat. When you see a net, try to imagine folding it back up into its original 3D shape.

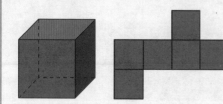 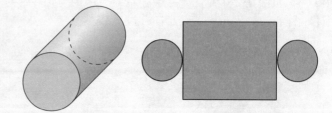

SATs practice

 Complete the table.

	Number of faces
cone	
cube	
sphere	
cylinder	

 Which of the following are correct nets for a cuboid? Put a tick inside them.

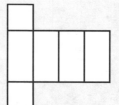 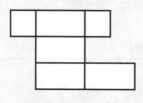 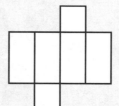 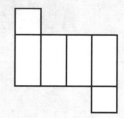

 Here is a cube with a hole through the middle of it.

Draw on the net where the two holes could be.

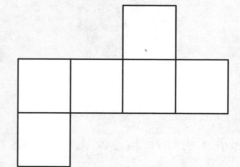

3D shape problems

As well as knowing the names of 3D shapes, you also need to know the names of the different parts of the shape.

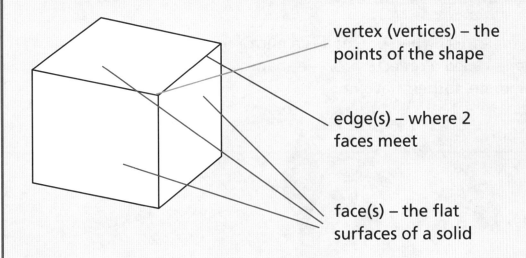

vertex (vertices) – the points of the shape

edge(s) – where 2 faces meet

face(s) – the flat surfaces of a solid

SATs practice

 Complete the table.

	Number of faces	Number of edges
cone		1
cube	6	
sphere		0
cylinder		

 How many vertices does a cube have? _____

5 Complete the table.

	Number of edges	Number of vertices
cuboid		
square-based pyramid		
triangular prism		
tetrahedron		

Geometry

Symmetry and reflection

An object is symmetrical when one half is a mirror image of the other half. This is sometimes called a reflection. Some shapes or objects have more than one line of symmetry; others have none.

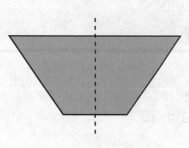

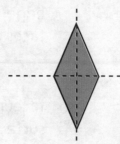

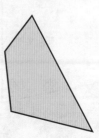

1 line of symmetry
(mirror line)

2 lines of symmetry
(2 mirror lines)

zero lines of
symmetry

Sometimes in questions you will be asked to draw 'about' the mirror line. This just means that when you have finished, the drawing should look the same both sides of the mirror.

SATs practice

 Using a ruler, complete the diagram below to make a symmetrical shape about the mirror line.

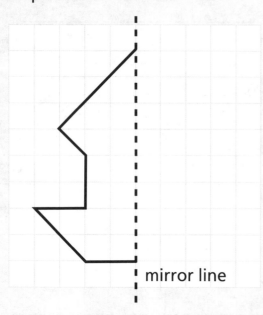

mirror line

SATs practice

 Using a ruler, draw the reflection of this shape.

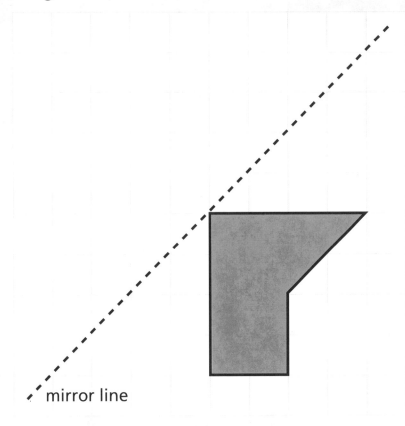

mirror line

The diamond below has two lines of symmetry. Write down the coordinates of C and D.

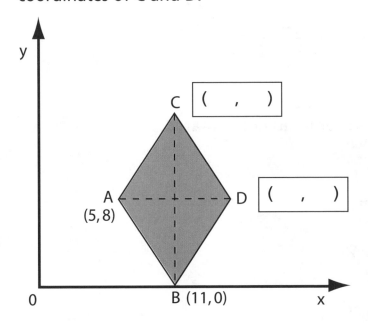

Rotation and translation

A shape can be rotated about a stationary point in either a clockwise or anticlockwise direction. This is called a rotation.

When a shape is moved without turning or reflecting it, this is called a translation.

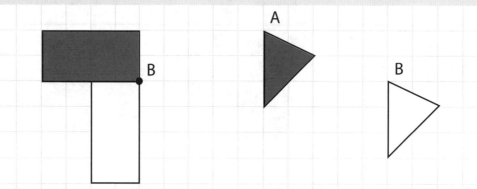

The red rectangle has been rotated anticlockwise about point B.

The red triangle has been translated from point A to point B.

SATs practice

 This three-way arrow is rotated 90° clockwise.

Put a tick inside the shape after it has been rotated.

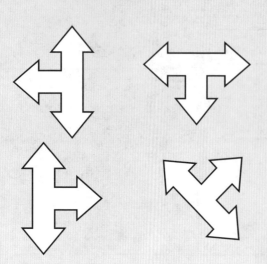

Now practise what you have learnt.

SATs practice

 Using a ruler, draw the shape below rotated by 90° in a clockwise direction about point B.

B

 Here is a pentagon on a grid. The pentagon is translated so that point A becomes point B. Using a ruler, draw the new pentagon.

A

•B

Coordinates

Basic coordinates

Coordinates are pairs of numbers or letters on a grid or map used to show the positon of something.

The first number is always along the *x* or horizontal axis.

The second number is always along the *y* or vertical axis.

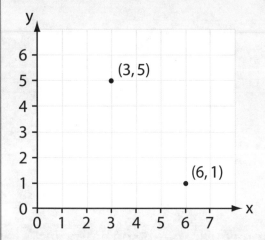

In order to remember which axis to go along first, use one of these phrases to help:

Along the corridor and up the stairs.

Along the runway and up into the air.

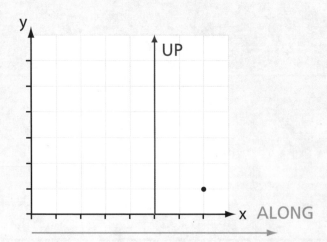

Now practise what you have learnt.

SATs practice

 Write down the coordinates of points A, B and C.

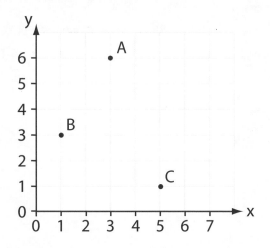

| A = (,) | B = (,) | C = (,) |

 Look at the coordinate grid above. A, B and C are three corners of a rectangle. What are the coordinates of the fourth corner?

(,)

 Here is a parallelogram.

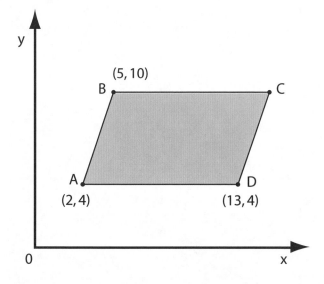

Write the coordinate of point C.

C = (,)

Coordinates

Advanced coordinates

Sometimes we use negative numbers on coordinate grids. These work exactly the same as positive coordinates. Just always remember to read the *x* axis first and then the *y* axis.

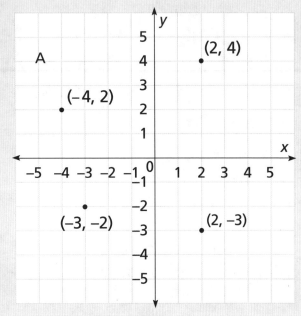

SATs practice

LEVEL 5 A, B and C are three points of a rectangle.

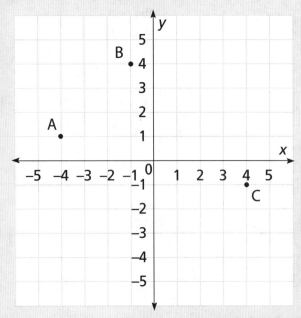

Write the coordinates of the fourth point. (　　,　　)

Angles

Types of angles

An angle is how far something turns. If a whole turn is completed, then the angle turned is a 360° turn.

There are a few different types of angles that you need to know.

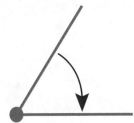

An **acute** angle is between 0° and 90°.

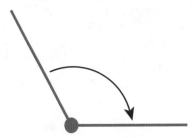

An **obtuse** angle is between 90° and 180°.

A half turn or **straight line angle** is 180°.

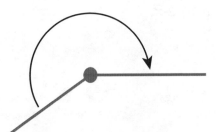

A **reflex** angle is between 180° and 360°.

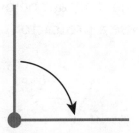

A quarter turn or **right angle** is 90°.

Angles

Types of angles (continued)

Now practise what you have learnt.

SATs practice

 Join the dots up to make a 4-sided shape with only 2 right angles.

LEVEL 4 Estimate the size of angle *x*.
(Do **not** use a protractor.)

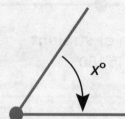

$x =$ ___ °

LEVEL 5 Look at the diagram below. Calculate angle *x*.
(Do **not** use a protractor.)

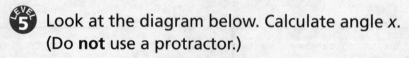

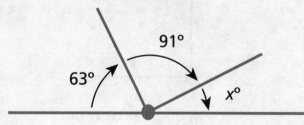

63°   91°   *x*°

Measuring angles

Angles are measured using a protractor or angle measurer.

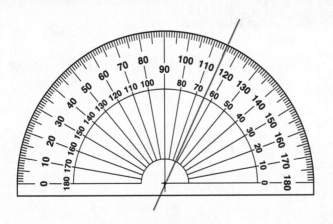

SATs practice

 Measure angle *y* accurately. Use a protractor.

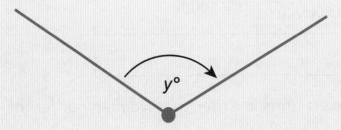

y =	°

5 Draw accurately an isosceles triangle with 2 angles of 40°.
Use a ruler and a protractor.
The first line has been drawn for you.

Units of measure

Units of measure and converting

Length, weight and capacity are all measured in different units. These can be seen in the table below:

Key
mm = millimetres   g = grams   ml = millilitres
cm = centimetres   kg = kilograms   cl = centilitres
m = metres   l = litres
km = kilometres

Length	Weight	Capacity
1cm = 10mm	1kg = 1000g	1cl = 10ml
1m = 100cm	1 tonne = 1000kg	1l = 1000ml
1km = 1000m		

You will need to be able to convert units in order to solve many different sorts of problems.

Example

How many millimetres in 32 centimetres?

There are 10mm in 1cm, so we need to multiply the number of centimetres by 10 to find the number of millimetres.

$$32 \times 10 = 320$$

Answer: There are 320 millimetres in 32 centimetres.

SATs practice

LEVEL 3 How many centimetres are there in 2 metres?

_____ cm

LEVEL 4 How many millilitres are there in $\frac{3}{4}$ l?

_____ ml

LEVEL 5 Dennis buys a 2 kilogram bag of flour to bake some bread. Each loaf of bread requires 150 grams of flour to make it. How many loaves of bread can Dennis make with the flour?

| | loaves |

More SATs practice

LEVEL 3 How many kilograms are there in four tonnes?

_____ kgs

LEVEL 4 How many centilitres are there in 3.7 litres?

_____ cl

LEVEL 5 Richard needs 150ml of orange cordial to make 2l of orange drink. A bottle of orange cordial is 750ml. How many litres of orange drink can Richard make if he uses a whole bottle of orange cordial?

| | litres |

Scales

Reading scales

Scales are the markings on containers, dials or even rulers that show you how much there is of something. It is important to look carefully at the scale in order to work out what the markings on it represent.

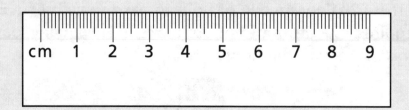

On this scale each centimetre is marked, but there are also markings between each centimetre, which are 1mm apart.

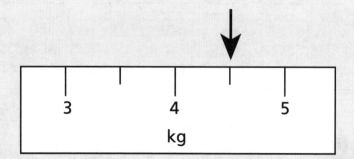

Similarly, on this scale each kilogram is marked, but there are also markings half way between each kilogram which represent $\frac{1}{2}$ kg, which is equivalent to 500g. The arrow on this scale is pointing to $4\frac{1}{2}$ kg, which is equal to 4 kg and 500g.

Now practise reading scales.

SATs practice

 Look at the measuring jug below. How much liquid is in the measuring jug?

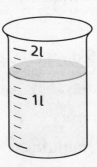

[   ] ml

 Look at the measuring jug below. How much more liquid do we have to add to make 380ml of liquid?

[   ] ml

 Jake weighs some sugar on his scales.

a How many grams of sugar does Jake have?　　　　[   ] g

b If Jake needs 350g of sugar altogether, how much more sugar does he need to add?　　[   ] g

Time

Time and the calendar

Here are some basic facts about the calendar that you need to know.

1 year = 365 days (366 days in a leap year)

1 week = 7 days

1 day = 24 hours

1 hour = 60 minutes

1 minute = 60 seconds

You also need to know the names of the months of the year and how many days are in each month.

January (31)

February (28*)

March (31)

April (30)

May (31)

June (30)

July (31)

August (31)

September (30)

October (31)

November (30)

December (31)

* February has 29 days in a leap year.

SATs practice

 a How many hours are there in two days?

_____ hours

b How many days are there altogether in November and December?

_____ days

 Here is a calendar for October 2008.

October 2008

Sun	Mon	Tues	Wed	Thur	Fri	Sat
			1	2	3	4
5	6	7	8	9	10	11
12	13	14	15	16	17	18
19	20	21	22	23	24	25
26	27	28	29	30	31	

a The school disco is on the third Friday in the month.
What is the date of the school disco?

_____

b Bonfire night is on the 5th of November.
On which day of the week in 2008 is bonfire night?

_____

Time

Analogue and digital time

As well as knowing how to tell the time using a traditional, analogue clock, you should also be able to tell the time using a digital clock. Digital clocks can be either 12-hour clocks or 24-hour clocks.

If 8.25 is converted to the 24-hour clock, the times would be:

Morning 08:25   (we just put a 0 in front of the 8)

Evening   20:25   (we need to add twelve to the 8)

SATs practice

 Match the clock to the correct digital time.

17:05

23:20

07:00

12:45

a Sally and Ross sat down to watch a DVD.
The DVD started at 15:50 and finished at 17:25.
How long did the DVD last?

_____

b If Sally and Ross had started watching the DVD at 6.30pm, what time would the DVD have finished?

_____

5 Here is part of a bus timetable.

	Bus 1	Bus 2	Bus 3	Bus 4
London	10:10	-	12:10	13:10
Reading	11:08	11:30	-	-
Birmingham	12:25	-	-	15:21
Manchester	-	14:45	15:38	17:15
Liverpool	15:22	16:23	-	18:47

How long does the second bus from Reading take to get to Liverpool?

┌─────────────────────────────────────┐
│   │
│   │
│   │
│   │
│   │
│   │
│   ┌──────────┐ │
│   │   │ │
└──────────────────────────┴──────────┴─┘

Perimeter and area

Perimeter

The perimeter of a shape is the distance all the way round the edge.

To find out the perimeter of this shape, you just have to add together the lengths of all four sides:

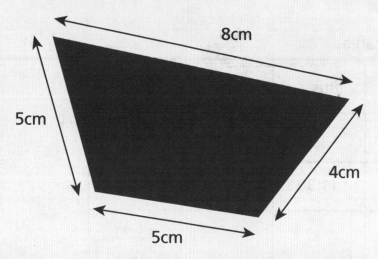

Perimeter = 8cm + 5cm + 5cm + 4cm = 22cm

The perimeter of this shape looks a bit trickier, but all you have to do is to add all the lengths of the sides up!

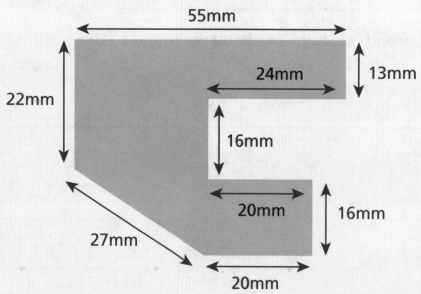

Perimeter = 55mm + 13mm + 24mm + 16mm + 20mm + 16mm + 20mm
+ 27mm + 22mm

= 213mm or 21.3cm

SATs practice

 A rectangular playground measures:

56.5m

37m

What is the perimeter of the playground? _____

 A regular hexagon has a perimeter of 42cm.
What is the length of each side?

_____

 A rectangle has a length of 26.2cm.

26.2cm

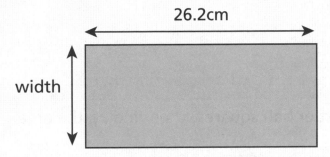

width

The perimeter of the rectangle is 80cm.

Calculate the width of the rectangle.

cm

Perimeter and area

Area

The area of a shape is the size a surface takes up. It is measured in square units.

If a shape is drawn on square paper, it is easy to find the area. Just add up the number of squares.

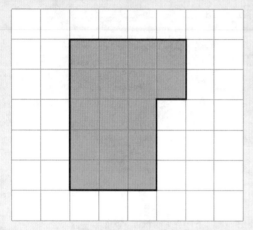

This shape has an area of 17 square units.

If this was a cm square grid, the area of the shape would be 17cm^2.

You just need to count the number of shaded squares!

Sometimes you have to count part or half squares when finding the area.

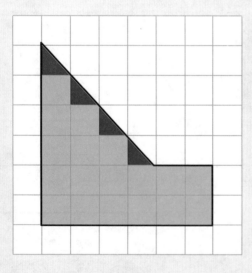

In this shape the whole squares shaded in green add up to 18. There are also 4 half squares shaded in red which add to 2. So the area of the shape is:

18 + 2 = 20

SATs practice

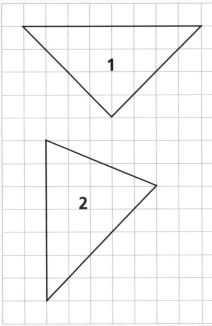

Work out the area of these two triangles.

Triangle 1 [_____] squares

Triangle 2 [_____] squares

4 On the grid draw a rectangle that has the same area as the shaded shape.

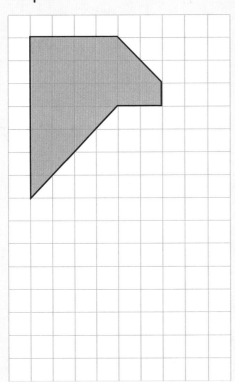

5 A rectangle measures 13cm by 16cm. What is the area of the rectangle?

[_____]

[_____] cm²

Probability

Chance and outcome

Probability is the **chance** that a particular **outcome** will occur.

Probability can be recorded on a scale of 0 to 1, showing the likelihood or chance that a particular outcome will occur.

On this scale, 0 means impossible and 1 means certain.

Probability can also be written as a fraction:

$$0.1 = \frac{1}{10} \qquad 0.25 = \frac{1}{4} \qquad 0.5 = \frac{1}{2} \qquad 0.75 = \frac{3}{4}$$

What is the probability of rolling a 6 when you roll a dice, for example?

With each roll there are 6 possible outcomes, in that you could roll a 1, 2, 3, 4, 5 or 6. So, if you roll the dice once, the probability that you will roll a 6 is a 1 chance out of 6, or $\frac{1}{6}$.

Similarly, if you toss a coin, the chance of it landing on a head is a 1 chance out of 2, or $\frac{1}{2}$, because there are 2 sides to your coin.

Now practise what you have learnt.

SATs practice

3 There are 10 coloured balls in a bag: 7 red balls, 2 green balls and 1 white ball.

If you put your hand in the bag and randomly choose a ball, which colour ball are you least likely to pull out?

_____

4 Here is a spinner which is a regular octagon.

Which two numbers are equally likely to come up?

☐ and ☐

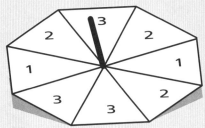

5 Here is a box of different coloured tiles.

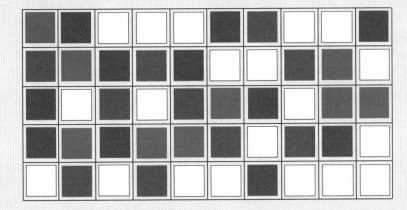

The tiles are taken out of the box at random.

What is the probability of getting a white tile? Write your answer as a fraction.

$\dfrac{\boxed{}}{\boxed{}}$

Tables, charts and graphs

Bar charts

A bar chart uses vertical or horizontal bars to represent quantities on a graph. You will be asked questions to see if you understand the charts.

Example

In a zoo there are 8 monkeys, 6 lions, 4 elephants and 10 merecats. This can be shown in the following two ways.

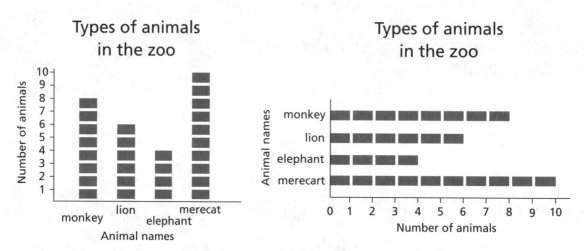

What is the most common animal in the zoo?

How many more lions than elephants are there?

Answer: The biggest bar on the chart is the merecat's, so the most common animal in the zoo is the merecat.
There are 6 lions and 4 elephants, so there are 2 more lions than elephants.

SATs practice

 This chart shows the amount of pocket money some children got each week.

How much pocket money did Joe get?

———————————————

How much more pocket money did Holly get than Liz?

———————————————

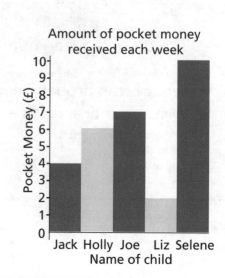

The number of points two teams got in each of the last five football seasons is shown on the chart below.

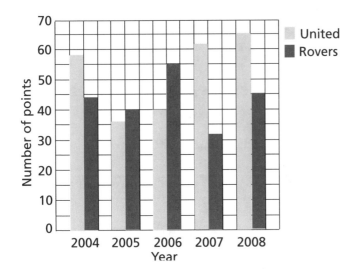

How many points did Rovers get in 2004? _____

In which year was there the greatest difference in points between the two teams? How many points difference was there?

year _____ points _____

 Some children took an end of year spelling test. The graph below shows the length of time it took the children to complete the test.

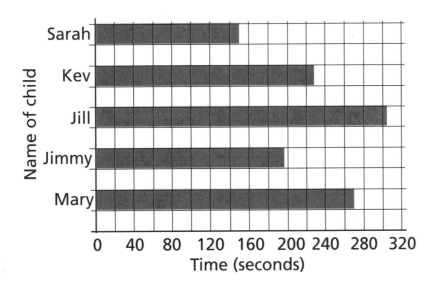

a How long did it take Sarah to complete the test?

_____ secs

b Estimate how much longer Jill took than Jimmy.

_____ secs

Tables, charts and graphs

Picture graphs

A picture graph is a graph which uses pictures or symbols to represent a quantity.

The graph below shows the number of pizzas that were delivered over the course of a week.

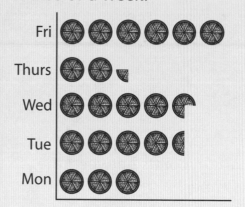

You will be asked questions to see if you understand the picture graph.

Example

How many pizzas were sold on Wednesday?

Answer: There are 4 and $\frac{3}{4}$ pizza symbols by Wednesday. This means that 16 (4 × 4) + 3 ($\frac{3}{4}$ of 4) pizzas were sold on Wednesday, which comes to 19 altogether.

SATs practice

 The graph below shows the number of hours of sunshine in a week in August.

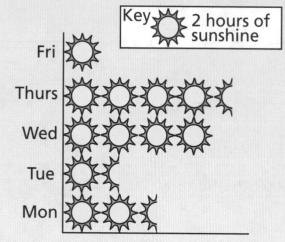

a How many hours of sunshine were there on Monday?

_____ hours

b How many hours of sunshine were there altogether on Tuesday and Wednesday?

_____ hours

The numbers of tickets sold for a pop concert are shown on the graph below.

Fri

Thurs

Wed

Tue

Mon

Key

[ADMIT ONE] = 500 tickets

Estimate how many tickets were sold on these days.

a Tuesday _____ tickets

b Wednesday _____ tickets

 Look at the graph above.

Estimate how many more tickets were sold on Thursday than Monday.

| | tickets |

Tables, charts and graphs

Pie charts

A pie chart (or pie graph) is a chart which uses a circle divided into sections. Each section then represents a part of the total.

The pie chart below shows the colour of children's eyes from a class of 30 children in a school.

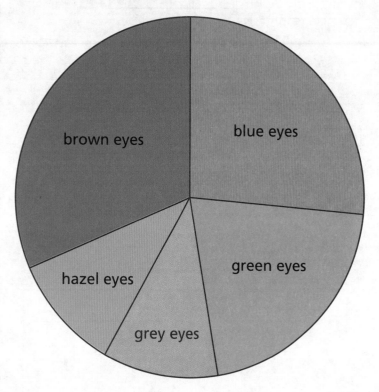

You will be asked questions to see if you understand the pie chart.

Example

What fraction of children's eyes are brown?

Estimate the total number of children with blue or grey eyes.

Answer: Approximately $\frac{1}{3}$ of the children's eyes are brown.
If you put the parts of the pie that are blue and grey together, it is about a $\frac{1}{3}$. There are 30 children altogether, so the calculation you need to do is $\frac{1}{3}$ of 30. The answer is approximately 10 children.

Classes 3 and 4 did a survey of their favourite flavour of crisps.

The pie chart below shows their results.

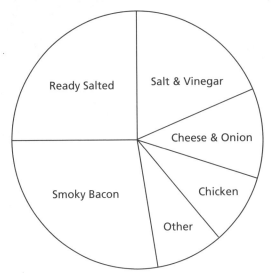

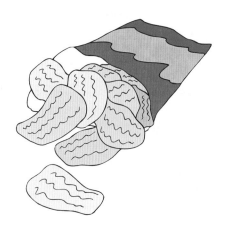

a Estimate what fraction of the crisps are Salt & Vinegar.

b There were 60 children surveyed altogether.
Estimate how many children had Ready Salted as their favourite.

Tables, charts and graphs

Line graphs

A line graph (or line chart) uses lines to join points which represent data. Most line graphs have numbers on both the *x* axis and the *y* axis.

The graph below shows the temperature of water as it is heated up. The temperature was taken every 30 seconds.

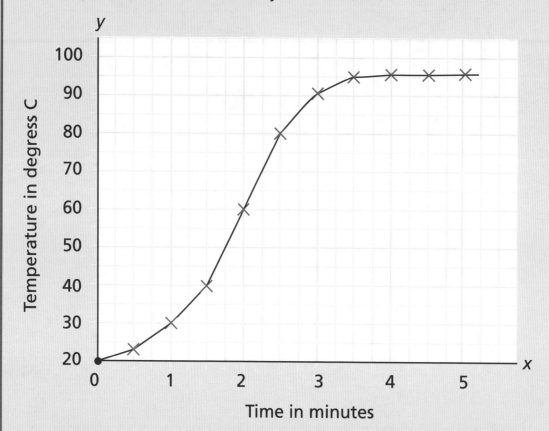

You will be asked questions to see if you understand the line graph.

Example

What was the temperature of the water after 3 minutes?

How long did the water take to rise from 40°C to 80°C?

Answer: Look along the *x* axis to 3 minutes, go vertically up until you reach the curve. By looking across at the *y* axis it is easy to see that the water temperature after 3 minutes was 90°C.

The time at 40°C was approximately 1 minute 30 seconds and at 80°C it was 2 minutes 30 seconds, so the water took 1 minute to rise from 40°C to 80°C.

Some people went on a sponsored walk up a mountain. They measured how far up the mountain they went every hour.

The results are shown on the graph below.

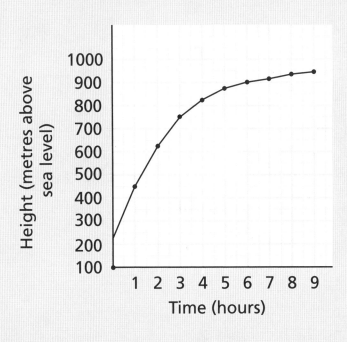

a How high above sea level were the people after 3 hours?

_____ m

b How many metres did the people climb between 1 and 6 hours?

_____ m

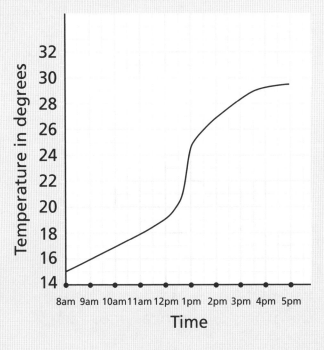 This graph shows the temperature in a conservatory on a sunny day.

a Estimate the temperature at 11:30am.

_____ °C

b Estimate the time that the temperature reached 28°C.

_____ pm

Averages

Mode, mean and median

There are three types of averages you need to consider.

1 Mode   **2** Mean   **3** Median

The most common type of average used is the mean, but sometimes the mode or median are used too. It is important to know which average someone is talking about, as the answers can be significantly different in some cases.

For instance, take this set of eleven numbers, written in order.
What is the average?

5, 12, 13, 18, 32, 35, 40, 40, 40, 115, 200

The mode is 40, the mean is 50 and the median is 35.

Mode

The mode is the most frequently occurring number in a set of numbers.

Example

Here are six children's shoe sizes.

Alex	4
Danny	3
Ella	4
Heather	6
Nicole	2
John	5

The mode of these numbers is 4 because 4 appears twice in the list and the others only appear once each.

SATs practice

Here are the heights of some children.

134cm 140cm

 126cm  126cm

 117cm

137cm  130cm

Natalie Callum   Kerry   Harry   Jane   Jake   Sue

What is the mode of these heights?

_____ cm

Here are the heights of some children.

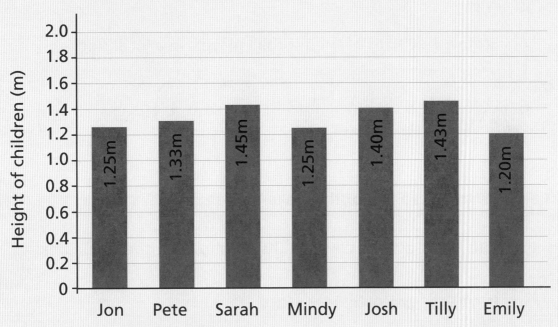

What is the mode of these heights?

_____

Averages

Mean

The mean is one type of average of a set of numbers.
To find the mean of a set of numbers:
1 Find the sum of the set of numbers.
2 Divide the sum by the number of numbers in the set.

Example

Here are 6 numbers.

23   8   15   30   17   21

To find the mean of these numbers, add all the numbers together and then divide by how many numbers there are:

$(23 + 8 + 15 + 30 + 17 + 21) \div 6 = 19$, so 19 is the mean.

SATs practice

 Look at the shoe sizes of the football players in a local side.

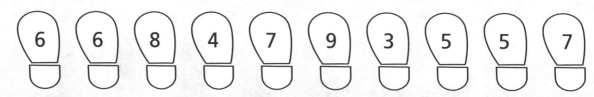

Calculate the mean size of the players' boots. _____

Billy rolls a dice 20 times. His results are shown in the graph below.

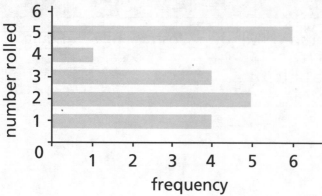

Calculate the mean number rolled on the dice. _____

Median

Median just means mid-point. To find the median of a set of numbers, you must first put the numbers in order and then find the number or numbers which are in the middle.

Example

Here are 9 numbers.

21   35   45   22   8   15   127   87   61

First, put them in order.

8   15   21   22   35   45   61   87   127

So 35 is the median of this set of numbers.

SATs practice

4 Look at the set of numbers below and circle the median number.

34   41   69   70   108   200   210   587   588

5 Look at the numbers below.

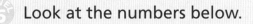

5   13   30   1   19   14   17   8   19   4
8   29   21   7   11   13   18   2   24   22
30

What is the median number?

Notes